CHERISHED
Memories
LONG of AGO

Douglas Jones

NEWMAN SPRINGS PUBLISHING
320 Broad Street
Red Bank, NJ 07701

First originally published by Newman Springs Publishing 2023

ISBN 979-8-88763-230-8 (Paperback)
ISBN 979-8-88763-231-5 (Digital)

Printed in the United States of America

Cherished Memories of Long Ago

06/14/2022

My story starts when I was born in Los Angeles, California. Mom had to walk a couple of blocks to the hospital where I was born.

Not long after that, we moved to Auburn, California. My grandpa was the manager of a lumber company. The company owned the house where Grandpa and Grandma lived. Mom, Dad, and I lived there for a few years.

Dad was driving a cab and eventually joined the army. He got orders to go to Fort Knox in Kentucky. Mom and I joined Dad, and I believe I was about three years old.

We lived not too far from Fort Knox on an old country road. I remember Mom and me walking to the country store. To me, it seemed like it took forever to get there. Mom got a job as a waitress at a truck stop called the Rogersville Inn.

We eventually moved closer to the truck stop on the highway. Mom never owned a car, so she always walked to work.

Me and Mom standing in front of Grandpa and
Grandma's house in Auburn, California.

When Dad wasn't doing army duties, he would emcee nightclubs, and he was on a local radio station at Fort Knox.

Dad met a German lady while singing on the radio station, and they would sing songs together. As the story goes, they got hooked up. Mom and Dad got divorced. Mom had me for nine months during school, and Dad had me for three months.

Dad finally left Kentucky. He got stationed somewhere else. I have no idea where. I was eight years old when all this took place. Mom met someone and eventually got married. We moved to my stepdad's parents' home, which was way out in the sticks in Red Hill, Kentucky.

There was no electricity and no running water. We had to walk about a quarter mile down a hill to get water from a cistern. Priming it was fun.

Out in the country, not too far from where we lived, was a one-room schoolhouse. Someone bought the schoolhouse and wanted to turn it into a regular house. My grandpa (my stepdad's dad) was a carpenter, so he was hired to convert it into a house.

I helped where I could. The people who bought the old schoolhouse had a large family.

I became friends with one of the boys, and we played cowboys and Indians. On Saturday mornings, I would watch TV. I guess it was the first television I had ever seen.

The railroad tracks were not too far from my friend's house. I remember me and my friend sitting on the bank overlooking the tracks. The train would stop where we were sitting, and some of the workers would get out of the caboose and give us apples and oranges.

Trains don't have cabooses anymore. One day, we were playing in the field close to the tracks when a train came by, and a spark from one of its wheels landed in the field and started a fire.

The fire was headed toward the woods, and there were homes to consider, and the town of Vine Grove would be in the path of the fire.

We had small hatchets, so we cut down a couple of small cedar trees and proceeded to put the fire out. With our singed eyebrows and black faces, we put the fire out before it reached the woods.

This incident was never told. One time, Mom had to go to the country store, and it had been snowing. We decided to take a shortcut through the woods.

On the way home, the snow had covered our tracks, so we got lost. We finally saw this fence that bordered the property and followed it till we came to an opening in the fence.

We were close to the house. We made it. It seemed like we had been walking for hours. Sometimes Mom would let me camp out in the woods only if I could keep the house in view. I would go to the country store and buy tobacco, Bull Durham.

The pouch was only five cents, and the paper was a penny. There were twenty small papers for rolling the tobacco. I would camp out in the woods and roll my own tobacco and smoke. I was only nine years old when I started smoking.

I was never alone because Grandpa and Grandma had a big black dog that was always with me, and Mom always put the lamp in the window so I could keep the house in view.

The farm was sold, and we moved to Vine Grove, Kentucky. A quaint little town, it had a firehouse, a post office, a bank, a drugstore, a five-and-ten-cent store, a café (where my mom worked), a hardware store, and a couple of funeral homes.

The town had a public school and a Catholic school.

This is Betty Lou, her mom, and Baby S. Step on the back porch of my grandparents' house in Vine Grove.

This is Ruby. She lived next door. We were like brother
and sister. Her mom took us to see the first Elvis
Presley movie at the Knox Drive-in Theater.

This is Peggy and her two brothers. They lived next door in Vine Grove.

This is me, my dog Frosty, and Grandma Knapp. This is in
the front yard of their home in Vine Grove, Kentucky.

There were a couple of hardware stores, service stations, and pool halls. That's where I hung out.

The house the family bought had two rooms and a basement. Mom, my stepdad, and I slept in the basement.

In the meantime, my stepdad's brother was having s house built in the country. He and his wife lived in a trailer till the house was built.

Mom bought that trailer and moved it onto the property. The trailer had a bedroom at one end, and in the middle was the kitchen. At the other end was a couch and a small TV. I slept on the couch.

Our next-door neighbors had a big family. As a matter of fact, we were so close that we were just like family.

Ruby was next to the oldest, and we would play cowboys and Indians. Peggy was next, and we always would tease each other. The two boys were too young, and the oldest girl was dating. I was always invited to go over in the evenings and watch TV with them.

I called Peggy on the phone and talked to her, but she doesn't remember me.

I was told she has a hard time remembering things now. Another family would visit Grandma and Grandpa.

The young girl was Betty Lou. In the wintertime, we would make a snowman and throw snowballs at each other. We had such a good time. I carried her baby sister in my arms. We were just like family. I loved it.

Mom got a job at the café in Vine Grove. I remember that every payday, Mom would take me to the clothing store and buy me a shirt or a pair of pants for school. Then after three months, when school started, I had new clothes to wear. Back in the fifties, tips weren't that good.

Every night after work, Mom would put her tips on the dresser—nickels, dimes, quarters, all in separate stacks.

That's pretty much what we lived on. I was going to a public school, and my stepdad's mom (whom I will call Grandma) was a strong Catholic.

After a few years, the family wanted to send me to the Catholic school in Vine Grove. The school only went to the eighth grade.

I was not a Catholic, but the family got me into the school. There was a bully in the school that the kids were afraid of. One day, when recess was over and we were heading back to class, this bully came up behind me and kicked me in the behind. I turned around and punched him in the mouth. Late at lunchtime, he was sitting across from me, and with a mean look, he said to me, "Give me the ketchup."

Ketchup and other condiments had just come out in squeeze bottles, so I gave it to him all over his face. The head sister was standing at the table. She called Mom and told her what I had done. The head sister said she wanted to laugh.

Anyway, I didn't get in any trouble. I was just told not to do that again. I graduated in 1957 out of the eighth grade.

During the harvest season, the farmers in the area would hire me. I cut and cured tobacco, baled hay, and worked in the cornfields.

One time, I was hired to cut weeds in a cornfield. It was about twenty acres, so I got my hoe, my file, and a jug of water.

The farmer came and fetched me for lunch. During lunch, the farmer, his wife, and I sat in their dayroom and watched soap operas on TV. I was fifteen years old.

I had a cousin by marriage who was having a hard time with his dad. We were always talking about going to California. One morning, while I was asleep on the couch, I was roused by a knock at the door.

It was my cousin. He had a falling out with his dad. He wanted to go to California.

I said, "Are you serious?" He was very serious. After giving it some thought, I agreed.

We got together all the money that we had—nine dollars and forty cents (ha ha). I had a map of the United States, so we mapped out a route.

We would go to Tennessee into Arkansas and down into the Texas Panhandle. Then it was on to Pecos, El Paso, and Arizona till we arrived in California. Our destination was Auburn, California. We took the long way, but really, it only took us ten days.

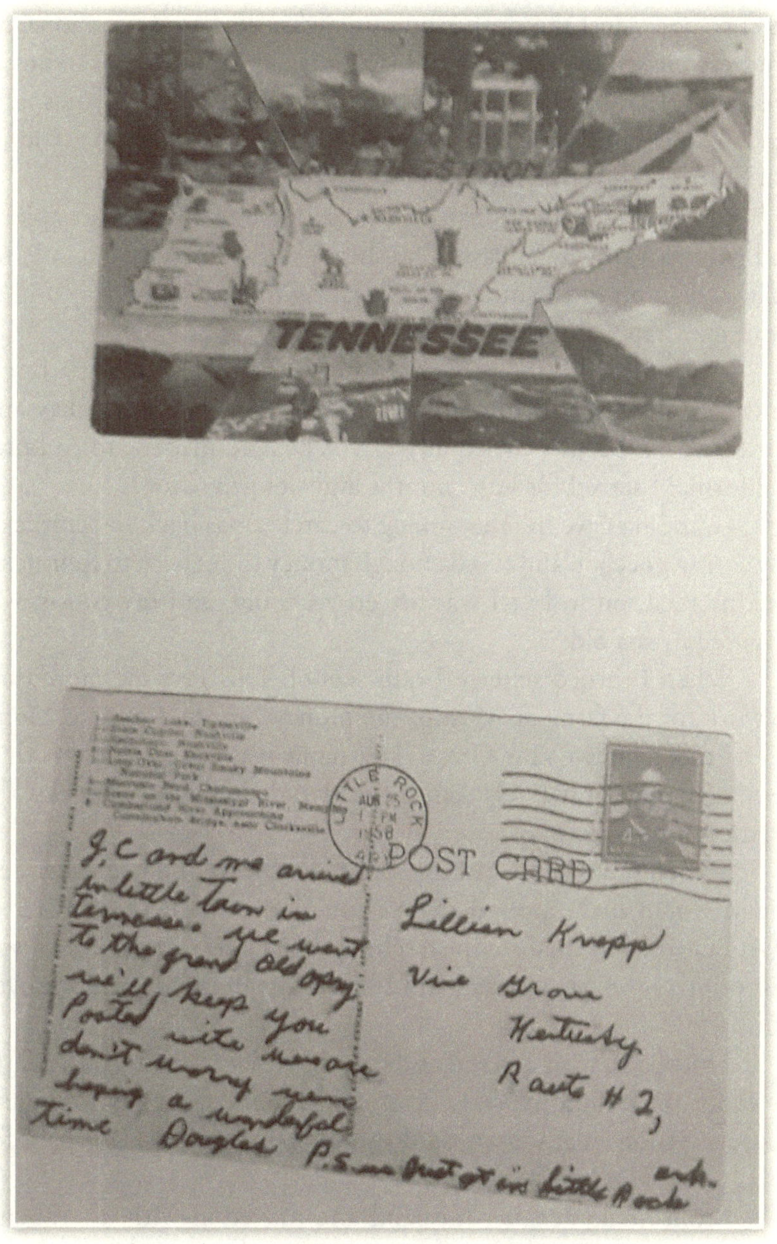

This is the postcard I sent Mom when hitchhiking
to California from Kentucky.

Oh, I forgot to mention, we hitchhiked. We left with no water and no food—just the clothes on our backs. We had quite a journey. We were chased by a carload of black guys in Little Rock, Arkansas. We caught a ride with AWOL soldiers, got chased by coyotes, and got put in jail in Pecos, Texas. The sheriff's office called my grandma in California to verify our story.

The next day, they turned us loose, gave us five dollars apiece, and gave us a ride to El Paso. The sheriff's office also gave us a letter of introduction to the other states, stating that we were okay and to let us go on to California.

I sure wished I had kept that letter. When I was in Little Rock, Arkansas, I did send Mom a postcard telling her we were okay and not to worry. Mom worried anyway. When we made it to Auburn, California, I stayed for four months and went to school.

Grandma gave me the money to catch a bus back to Kentucky. My cousin got a job and saved enough money to get back to Kentucky. I didn't mention it, but I was fifteen years old, and my cousin was seventeen years old.

When I turned sixteen, I quit school. This gave me more time to work for the farmers. Most of the money I made, I gave to Mom.

I met a girl in Vine Grove. Her name was Linda. She was thirteen years old, and I was sixteen years old. I thought she was the prettiest girl in town.

Sometimes when I had my stepdad's car, I, Linda, and her best friend would drive around town or in the country. I asked her to marry me, but she had to finish school. Years later, she told me it was just puppy love. My stepdad and I had a disagreement, and I moved out.

I moved in with a friend and his family. He sharecropped a farm of about three hundred sixty acres, and I worked for my room and board. On the side, we would do some logging, and I got paid for that.

Mom finally left her husband and moved in with us. When I turned eighteen, I was going through some papers and found some of Dad's army information. I wrote Washington with the information I had. It had been ten years since I had seen or heard from Dad.

A couple of months later, I received a letter from Dad. He was stationed in Japan and was married to a Japanese woman. I had a half brother.

I was excited. Dad wanted to know if I would like to come to Japan. I wrote back with a yes. I told Mom that I was eighteen and it was time to leave.

Dad sent me the money for bus fare to California. I stayed with Grandpa for three months. I had to have a series of shots and a passport before I could go to Japan.

I finally made it to Japan. I was so happy to see Dad, his wife, and my brother. I went back to school in the ninth grade. Mom made it back to Auburn, California. She got a job as a waitress in a coffee shop. I only stayed in Japan for a year.

The year I spent in Japan was very interesting. My stepmom took me way up into the mountains to meet her brother and sister-in-law. They had two small children, a boy and a girl. They also owned a store. I couldn't speak Japanese, and they couldn't speak English. Akia left me there for two weeks.

Akia's brother took me to meet an English professor. This professor was Japanese and taught English in college, but he hadn't spoken English in twenty years. His house was huge. In the back room, there was a Buddha made of pure gold with a thousand arms.

I hated to leave Japan, but I had joined the army over there. I took my basic at Fort Ord in California in 1962. I had two weeks' leave, which I spent in Auburn, California, with my mom. After that, I was sent to Missouri. I was stationed in a small town called Pleasant Hill, Missouri.

The missile site was out in the boonies (or sticks), surrounded by four cornfields. It was during the Cuban crisis, and I didn't have security clearance, so I and three others pulled KP and guard duty for three months.

One Saturday night, I and a friend went to a barn dance. Pleasant Hill always had a barn dance on Saturdays.

I met a wonderful girl at the dance, and in a year, we were married. She had three young children from a previous marriage. I fell in love with them. Even today, they still call me Daddy Doug.

I was sent to Leavenworth, Kansas, to a missile site.

The missile site in Missouri was taken over by the National Guard. My firstborn son was born in the army hospital in Leavenworth, Kansas. Later, I received orders to go to Thule in Greenland.

My wife and kids moved back to Missouri to stay with her mom and dad.

The tour in Thule was a year, but after eight months, they closed all the missile sites.

I was sent to Nebraska, to another small town called Valparaiso, where I rented an apartment.

I bought an old Buick, drove down to Missouri, and got my wife and kids.

I don't remember how long I was stationed in Nebraska, but that missile site finally closed, and I was sent to Fort Bliss in Texas. My family went with me.

We rented a house not too far from the base. My wife's family came down from Missouri. We took them shopping and to the bullfights in Juarez, Mexico.

After some time, I received orders to go to Okinawa. I moved my family to Auburn, California. We rented a house not too far from downtown.

I finally made it to Okinawa. The island was very interesting. I and some of the guys went sightseeing. On the way down the hill, we had to go through a small village, and in the middle of the village was a big tree.

I asked one of the villagers who could speak English about the tree. He told me that years ago, a soldier raped a young girl from the village, so people in the village hung him from the tree. The tree was left in the middle of the village as a reminder.

There was a town called Naminoue. It had a couple of stores, cafes, and bars. I made friends with one of the bar owners. Sometimes she had her driver take me back to the missile site when the bar closed. I was so well known that they had a nickname for me. I was called the Naminoue Kid.

In 1968, someone by the name of Ronnie Fray wrote and recorded a song called "On the Road to Naminoue."

One time, when the town was off limits, I was walking down the street, and around the corner came the MPs (military police). They saw me, and the chase was on. I ran down an alley and tried to jump over a trash can. I must have passed out because when I woke up, I was lying on my back, and my legs were on top of the trash can. Anyway, I didn't get caught.

Another time, I got into an argument with the Okinawan police, and they beat me with their nightsticks. The military police stopped them, and I caught a cab back to the site. I could hardly walk or move for almost two weeks. We did our maneuvers at a place called Bolo Point.

One day, we were training for riot control. It was raining so hard, and we had ponchos, but our captain would not let us put them on. Boy, did we get drenched.

The colonel came to see how we were doing, and when he saw us without our ponchos, he chewed the captain out. After eighteen months, my tour was up. I was sent to Fort Bliss, Texas.

My wife and I were not getting along, so she and the kids moved back to Missouri. Later, we were divorced. I put in my papers to go back to Okinawa.

Six months later I was back in Okinawa. Everyone was glad to see me again. During one of our inspections, we loaded up a truck with things we didn't want the inspectors to see. There was a cave where we hid everything.

I was still drunk from the night before, so they hid me in the cave also. Ha ha. We passed the inspection. From my room, I could see the ocean, and off in the distance was a small island.

I was told it was a leper colony. After eighteen more months in Okinawa, I was stationed back at Fort Bliss, Texas.

I tried to go back to Okinawa for the third time, but the missile sites were closing, and the United States gave the Ryukyu Islands back to Japan.

I finally received orders to go to New Jersey. I met my second wife in New Jersey. She had two children, and she gave me a son and two daughters.

My last duty station was in Germany. It was a three-year tour. I took my wife and kids with me. We got housing off base.

The army at that time had some kind of law that if you didn't make E-6 by thirteen years, you had to get out of the army.

I was on the promotion list, but when that came out, I was taken off the list. They gave me two options: I could finish my tour in Germany or take an early out. I chose the early out. I had over thirteen years of service. I got out in 1976 with an honorable discharge.

I stayed in New Jersey for fifteen years. I worked at a place called Electronic Enclosures. They made cabinets for electronic devices and computers.

I also worked in security doing night watch in factories and high-rise buildings.

After fifteen years, I left New Jersey and moved back to California. My wife and I got divorced. I got a job working in a care facility. It was a very big place. It had senior housing, skilled nursing, and convalescent.

I met a very nice woman who was working at the facility. She had been married also. After our divorces were final, we were married. We have been married for thirty-one years now, and I haven't had a drink in thirty-two years. I was on Facebook one day and noticed that it said, "Do remember Vine Grove, Kentucky."

I started doing some research and saw a name that looked familiar. It was Betty Lou. I texted her, and in a few minutes, I received a text saying, "Where have you been?" I haven't talked to or seen her for sixty years. We had quite a reunion. We keep in touch with each other. Betty Lou gave me the phone number of another dear friend. Her name is Sue.

This is me and my wife today.

I have talked to her also. I have located my very first girlfriend, Linda.

She married her high school sweetheart, and they have been married for over fifty-five years. We keep in touch also. I now live here in Auburn, California, with my wife Sharon.

Both of us are going on eighty years old. Would you believe it! I don't know how much longer I will be around, but as long as I live, I will always cherish the memories of long ago.

Your Name

Douglas Jones
688 Mikkelsen Dr. #307, Auburn, California
95603 | (530) 320-9032 | dougiej43@gmail.com
08/20/2022

Dear Recipient,

I have a short story I would like published. It has 1,454 words. It's about a boy brought up in Kentucky, way out in the boonies. Thanks for your time.

Sincerely,
Douglas R. Jones

Life in the Country

This was in the early fifties. Being raised in the country was a good life. It was Mom, me, Grandpa, and Grandma. We lived so far back in the sticks that a rabbit had to carry its food on its back. Our farmhouse only had two rooms and an attic. Mom and I lived in the attic.

The bedroom Grandpa and Grandma occupied was also the living room. We had an old potbellied stove for heat, and there was a radio that we hooked up to a car battery. We had a wire on a pole that we used for an antenna.

The kitchen was the main part of the house. There was an old iron stove used for cooking. There were cupboards and a pantry and, of course, a table with chairs. Grandma sure could cook. She made the best blackberry cobbler.

We had to walk a good quarter mile down a hill to get our water. There was a cistern, and we had to prime the pump. It was a lot of fun in the winter. We had no electricity, no running water, and we pretty much lived off the land. There were collard greens and sassafras tea.

The sassafras bushes were dug up, and the root was boiled, and that made the tea. We had a very nice garden.

There was corn on the cob, tomatoes, green beans, onions, lettuce, cabbage, potatoes, and cucumbers. I can still see grandma sitting on the porch with a pan of green beans shucking them.

We hunted rabbits. We lived near the woods, and we also hunted squirrels. Once in a while, we would kill a deer. About once or twice a month, we would go into town to get supplies such as flour. Grandma loved to bake.

We had an apple orchard out back, and Grandma made the best apple pies. A couple of miles away, close to the railroad tracks, lived a man and woman who had a sorghum and molasses mill. Grandma would send me over there to get a jar of molasses.

Grandma made molasses candy. The molasses was great with butter on biscuits (yum-yum). We had a dog named Blacky. I don't know what kind of dog he was, but he was the best hunting dog I have ever seen.

Grandpa was still young enough to work. He worked at a distillery in Louisville, Kentucky.

They made whiskey such as Jack Daniels and Old Grand-Dad. Grandpa didn't drink while working, but when he came home, he was a little tipsy just from smelling the liquor.

Grandpa was getting ready to cut a piece of chewing tobacco off a twist. I asked him for a piece of tobacco because I wanted to try chewing and spitting like Grandpa. He gave me some, and as I started chewing, I swallowed it. Boy did I ever get dizzy and sick. I never tried that again. I just stuck to smoking tobacco, not chewing it.

It was such a joy living on the farm. We had sixty-five acres of rolling hills. Blacky and I played from one end of our land to the other end. When in the woods, I would play cowboys and Indians. Sometimes I would swing on vines and play Tarzan.

I would have to walk a good mile to the main road to catch the school bus. I enjoyed going to school, but I guess I just wanted to live in the country and enjoy life. Back in the fifties, life was simple.

I went fishing and frogging. And yes, I ate frog legs. You just had to keep them from jumping out of the frying pan. Ha ha.

Little red ants got in the flour bin. Grandma made biscuits for breakfast, and on the bottom of the biscuits, you could see little red specks. We ate the biscuits and couldn't taste the ants. I'm still alive, so it didn't bother us.

One time, Grandpa was cutting my hair with hand clippers. The clippers were pulling the hair on the back of my neck. I got up and started running out the screen door. Mom was right behind me. Well, the screen door had a very tight spring.

As I went out the screen door, it flew back and hit Mom in the face. I peeked around the corner and asked Mom, "Are you okay?" I won't repeat what Mom said to me. I didn't have many friends. I was the only child.

When I would get off the bus, I would take my shoes off. And as I walked home on our dirt road, I could feel the warm dirt between my toes.

There was also death. There was an older couple that lived not too far from where I caught the school bus. Her husband had passed away suddenly. We didn't have telephones back then, but they had an old fire bell. Boy did she ever ring that bell.

Grandpa went across the field to their home. Later, the funeral was held in the home.

On one occasion, we were plagued with a rat. Yes, one rat. This rat got into everything—the cupboards and even the stove in the kitchen. He even avoided the traps. One time, when Mom and I were upstairs in bed sleeping, we heard a sound like footsteps coming up the stairs.

Mom knew it was the rat. I was sleeping on a cot on the other end of the attic. Mom whispered to me and said, "Doug, get in bed with me. The rat is coming up the stairs."

When the rat was upstairs, we could see its shadow.

Mom whispered and said, "I hope he doesn't jump on the bed." About that time, it came and jumped on the bed. We screamed and I don't know who made it downstairs first. Anyway, someone told Grandpa to cover the trap with a dark cloth.

The rat was caught, and Grandpa burned it in the potbellied stove. No more rats. We enjoyed the evenings sitting around the radio, listening to country music.

Back then, it was Roy Acuff, Patsy Cline, Hank Williams, and Little Jimmy Dickens, just to name a few. On real hot nights, we would sit on the porch looking at the night sky and its wondrous beauty. The stars twinkled in the night sky, and the full moon shone when it appeared.

It was hard to see and do my homework under the lamplight, so I tried to do it before it got dark. Sometimes I would camp out in the woods. I made a lean-to for shelter, and Blacky was always with me. Mom put the lamp in the window so I could keep the house in view.

Grandpa built an outhouse, a two-seater (his and hers) with a picture window in the rear. Real fancy. We had a barn, but I think it was about to collapse.

We didn't do any farming. The land wasn't that good—the soil, I mean. We found a good spot for our garden, and that was about it. In the wintertime, we went sleigh riding, built snowmen, and threw snowballs.

Sometimes I would take the tractor into the woods and cut up some firewood for the stove. Winters were hard sometimes, but we made it through them. Mom had a job working at a restaurant.

We didn't have a car, so Mom either caught a ride or called the city cab. Grandpa always had a ride with one of his coworkers. We got around, but it was not easy.

We had a tractor but used it mostly to carry firewood in the winter. Sometimes the snow was so deep, the only way to get to the woods to get the firewood was to use the tractor.

Thinking back on those days, sometimes it would make me laugh. One time, a couple of old country boys came by to see us. They stayed a couple of hours. As they left and were on the far hill, we could barely see them.

One of the boys had to go to the bathroom, so he dropped his pants, and as he was squatting, the other boy pushed him into it. It was so funny, we were standing on the porch just dying with laughter.

I was picking blackberries one time and was chased by a bull. I think I jumped over a six-foot barbwire fence to get away. Ha ha. It seemed like it anyway.

Yes, living on the farm was good. Never a dull moment. I'm going on eighty years old now, but I still remember being raised in the country oh so many years ago.

Your Name

Douglas Jones
688 Mikkelsen Drive No. 307, Auburn, California 95603 | (530) 320-9032 | dougiej43@gmail.com
08/20/2022

Dear Recipient,

I have a short story I would like published. It has 1,997 words. It's about a boy who was brought up in a small town in Kentucky. Thanks for your time.

Sincerely,
Douglas R. Jones

My Life in a Small Country Town

I was brought up in a small town in Kentucky called Vine Grove. It was a quaint little town. Let's see. I believe it had a café. That's where my mom worked. The town had a bank, a grocery store, a clothing store, a five-and-ten-cent store, a drugstore, a post office, a fire station, a couple of service stations, some funeral homes, a hardware store, and, oh yes, a pool hall. That's where I hung out when I was old enough. I remember a theater where we only paid twenty-five cents to watch a movie.

There was a public school and a Catholic school and a Catholic church, and I believe there were a couple more churches, though I don't remember what denomination. Mom, me, and my stepdad lived in a trailer on his parents' property. For the first three years, I went to the public school, and since my stepdad's mom was a strong Catholic, I was sent to the Catholic school. It only went to the eighth grade, which I graduated from.

When I was still going to the public school, there were a couple of girls who were snitches. On one occasion, they saw me walk by the gym, and they went to the office and told them that I broke into the gym. I was sent to the office. Mr. Alton was our principal, and I had to see him.

He knew the girls were listening, so he got his paddle and said, "Every time I hit this chair, you holler." I did and we had a good laugh. I told him I didn't break into the gym, and he said, "I know you didn't." We had a good principal.

When I started going to the Catholic school, there was a bully. One day, when recess was over, he came up behind me and kicked me in the seat of my pants. I turned around and punched him in the mouth. At lunchtime, he sat right across from me and, with a mean look, said, "Give me the catsup." They had just come out with the squirt bottles, so I gave it to him—all over his face.

The head sister was standing by the table, and she sent for my mom. She told my mom what took place and said she could hardly keep from laughing. Anyway, I didn't get expelled, and the bully never bothered me again. I loved that town and the people in it.

I had two very good friends, Norman and Robert. When you saw one of us, you knew the other two were around. Later, they moved to Louisville, Kentucky.

There was a creek just below our house. I liked camping by the creek at night, listening to the sounds.

I knew this very sweet elderly woman named Essie. Her daughter was my teacher, and her name was Ms. Jacobs. Essie's husband got run over by a train, so she had me feed her horses every evening. She paid me a dollar, and she gave me cookies and ice cream. I remember Essie wore big-rimmed glasses, and she had an old black-and-white Chevy. When Essie was coming to town, someone would holler, "Here comes Essie!" Everyone would clear the street.

When I was old enough, I worked for the farmers in the area. The farmers paid me seventy-five cents an hour. When I was sixteen years old, I met a girl named Linda. She was thirteen. When I had my stepdad's car, I, Linda, and her best friend would ride around town or in the country.

My life was not so good. I lived in a trailer and slept on the couch. My stepdad was an alcoholic who could not hold down a job. Mom supported his habit. I remember he got hired at the Knox drive-in theater to clean up after the place was closed. He was usually passed out in his car, and I did the cleaning. My life was a mess. I didn't want Linda to see what I was going through in my life.

I finally just stopped seeing her. It has been sixty years or more, and I always wanted to tell her how sorry I was. To apologize. Well, I have apologized to Linda. She married her high school sweetheart, and they have been married for over fifty-five years. I'm so happy for her. She married a good man.

The railroad ran right through town. When the train went through town, I tried to count the cars. I found out that there was someone who did count the cars. It was his job to count the cars as they went through Vine Grove.

I remember one time I had to stay after school for getting in trouble. We lived way out in the country. The school bus I was supposed to be on had an accident. A truck ran through the side of the bus, killing one child and injuring others.

A girl that I knew would always save me a seat on the bus. We always sat in the first seat on the bus. She didn't get hurt, just got a bruise on her leg. The bus driver tried to warn everyone.

It was really bad. I had to walk home that night. It probably took me an hour or so. Mom heard what happened on the radio, and when I walked onto the porch, she was so relieved.

Being brought up in a small town like Vine Grove was really neat. The memories I have are of the good times. And there were bad times also, but I always want to remember the good times.

I had a good mom. When school was out for three months, every payday, Mom would take me to the clothing store and buy me a shirt or a pair of pants. When school started, I had clean clothes to wear every day.

When I was working for the farmers, I gave Mom most of the money I made.

I had a dog named Frosty. He was all white except for his head, which was black. He was given to me when he was a pup. My cat's name was CB.

We went to a barn dance one evening, and while I was sitting in the car, I saw this kitten. He was so small. I asked Mom if I could keep him.

She said I would have to ask the owner of the barn. So I did. He said I could have the kitten if I would name it after him. So I named him CB. CB lived a good life. He was a great barn cat. CB got run over by a car. I buried him way over in the field. I cried for at least two weeks or maybe more. Frosty lived a long time.

I had gone away for the weekend. When I came home, Frosty would always be there to greet me. Not this time. I never saw him again. I looked everywhere. My guess is he got into someone's henhouse and got shot. When they saw it was my dog, whoever it was probably buried him and never said anything.

At one time, we only had one policeman. Early one morning (it must have been around two), I was going through town in my stepdad's car. I was driving too slow and without a license. The police chief stopped me. He knew me and Mom. He followed me to our trailer and told Mom to take me to E-Town and get my license.

E-Town was a bigger city and the only place I could get my license at that time. E-Town was Elizabethtown, Kentucky. Anyway, I finally got my license.

The police chief left and went to another town. The township hired two policemen. One was tall, and the other one was short. We called the tall policeman Wyatt Earp, and the short policeman was Bat Masterson. They were young and a lot of fun.

When I turned sixteen, I was allowed in the pool hall—well, really, with a written statement from Mom and my stepdad. I started when I was fifteen. Back then, a game was only a dime. Sometimes I would only have a dime when I went into the pool hall, and I would walk out with the same dime. With a lot of practice, I got that good.

I have written two short stories. One is when I and my cousin hitchhiked from Kentucky to California about two thousand miles, and the other short story was a little bit about my life when I was born in California and moved to Kentucky and when I left. This story is about me and my friends in Vine Grove and the surrounding area.

The people in Vine Grove were good people—hardworking farmers. Most of them would give you the shirt off their back. Most of the kids were into scooters. I wanted a scooter, but Mom said no. She was afraid I would get hurt.

When I turned thirteen years old, Mom bought me a huffy bike. I rode that bike everywhere, way out in the country, where we first lived, and all over town. The price of gas was twelve or thirteen cents a gallon.

I remember buying gas for my stepdad's car, taking my girlfriend to the Knox Drive-in Theater, and buying popcorn and soda for less than seven dollars.

I remember the hot summers and the cold winters, but we made it through those bad times. I left when I turned eighteen, right around the year 1960. I returned in 1964 and in 1972 when I was in the army.

The year 1964 was the last time I saw my grandparents, and in 1974, I stayed with friends. I helped them sharecrop a farm before I left.

A couple of years ago, I was on Facebook, and it said, "Do remember Vine Grove, Kentucky." I joined that group and was looking for people whom I knew. I texted this one girl whose name looked familiar. She texted me right back. We keep in touch with each other.

Most of the friends that I knew are gone now. The ones that are still alive, I call and text.

I'm seventy-nine years old now, and I live in California. But I will always remember my life as a young boy in the small country town of Vine Grove, Kentucky.

Your Name

Douglas Jones
688 Mikkelsen Drive No. 307, Auburn, California 95603 | (530) 320-9032 | dougiej43@ gmail.com
08/20/2022

Dear Recipient,

I have a short story I would like published. It has 1,137 words. This is about a young boy (15) and a cousin (17) who hitchhiked two thousand miles or more from Kentucky to California in 1957. Thanks for your time.

Sincerely,
Douglas R. Jones

Ten Days

It was a typical morning in August 1958. I was sleeping on the couch in Mom's trailer with my dog lying at the foot of the couch. I heard a knock at the door; it was my cousin JC. JC and his dad got into an argument, and he was kicked out of the house. From time to time, we would talk about going to California. To me, I thought it was just talk. It would never happen. I was from California. Mom and I left California when I was about three years old to be with Dad. He was stationed at Fort Knox in Kentucky.

Mom and Dad got divorced. Dad finally left, leaving Mom and me behind to fend for ourselves. Mom remarried. I was eight years old then. But now I was fifteen years old, and JC was seventeen. JC asked me if I was ready to go to California. I said, "Are you serious?" His reply was yes. After giving it some thought, I agreed. We counted all the money we had—nine dollars and forty cents. I had a map of the United States, so we mapped out a route that we thought was the best way to go.

We took no food and no water, just the clothes on our backs. We had no idea how long it would take us, but off we went.

When we started hitchhiking, we were getting short rides, sometimes one or two miles. All those miles added up. We made a stop in Memphis, Tennessee, close to the Grand Ole Opry. We didn't have the money to go in, but we met an old railroad man. He told us a lot of stories about working on the railroad. We moved on. Later on, I found out that someone from Vine Grove went to the Grand Ole Opry and had seen us hitchhiking. They told Mom the next morning. Mom realized that we were going to California. That was the first day and night.

Mom was very worried about us, especially me. I remember getting to Little Rock, Arkansas. I sent Mom a postcard from Little Rock, telling her we were okay, not to worry, and that we went to the Grand Ole Opry, but we didn't. We were minding our own business when a car full of guys started chasing us. They were black, and we were very scared. We ran out into an open field where the grass was high. We lay low till they stopped looking for us. It seemed like it was hours, and we got out of the area as fast as possible.

We headed down to Texas. One night, to get out of the cold, we stopped at an all-night diner. The waitress on duty saw that we were hungry and cold. She fed us and let us sleep in her car till she got off work.

We started on our way. We had short-sleeve shirts, and in the desert at night, it got really cold. Some nights, we thought we would freeze to death. There were nights we would sleep on the ground, but we found out we could sleep on the back of billboards and get off the ground.

When we arrived in Pecos, Texas, we learned that the Red Cross was in Judge Roy Bean's historical building, the jailhouse. The Red Cross was giving out vouchers for food. They sent us to a restaurant downtown. We handed the waitress our vouchers and ordered breakfast. Little did we know that the sheriff was in the office with the owner of the restaurant. The waitress showed the vouchers to the owner and the sheriff. The sheriff came out and told us to come to his office when we finished eating.

After we ate, we proceeded to the sheriff's office. The police put us in separate rooms and interrogated us. We told them the truth. They put us in a cell, fed us, and washed our clothes. They called my grandma in California to check out our stories. Grandma told them to let us go. The next day, the sheriff's office released us, gave us five dollars apiece, and wrote a letter of introduction to the other states to let us go on to California.

The plainclothes police gave us a ride to El Paso. They let us out on the road, and we started hitchhiking again. Before we even got out of town, a soldier picked us up and took us to his house. He had three daughters about our age. They fixed us pancakes for breakfast and then washed and ironed our clothes. We stayed a couple of hours and went on our way.

We caught a ride with some soldiers that were AWOL. We were scared that we were going to get robbed or worse. We lucked out. They had a flat tire and had to stop at a service station to get it fixed. You should have seen us boys running to the highway to catch a quick ride before the tire was fixed. We did catch a quick ride.

One night, we were chased by a pack of coyotes. We were by a railroad, and a train was coming, so we ran across the tracks. That was how we got away from the coyotes. We walked for hours, and it was so cold. JC wanted to lie down and sleep, but I told him, "If we stop now, we will freeze to death." It must have been two o'clock in the morning—no cars, nothing. Just dark and cold.

Pretty soon, this lone car came up over the hill. It was a very nice-looking car. It stopped for us, and we were so happy. We did not know who was in the back seat sleeping or who was driving. We just knew that the car had a heater, and it was warm. After about a hundred miles, they took a different route. We stayed on the same road/route.

We caught another ride with a wrestler who was going to California to work on a ship. He took us all the way to Stockton, California. JC and I made it to my grandparents' house in Auburn, California. I went to school for four months, and Grandma paid my bus fare back to Kentucky. JC got a job and eventually made it back to Kentucky.

It was two thousand miles or more, but with everything we went through, it only took us ten days. We must have walked hundreds of miles. I was fifteen then, and I'm seventy-nine now. I don't think I want to go through that again.

Your Name

Douglas Jones
688 Mikkelsen Drive No. 307, Auburn, California 95603 | (530) 320-9032 | dougiej43@gmail.com
08/20/2022

Dear Recipient,

I have a short story I would like published. It has 1,209 words. This is when I was in the military in the late 1960s stationed in Okinawa, Japan. Thanks for your time.

Sincerely,
Douglas R. Jones

The Naminoue Kid

I joined the army in 1962 in Japan. My dad was stationed at Camp Zama in Japan. I took my basic at Fort Ord in California. The army sent me from California to Missouri, Kansas, Thule (Greenland), Nebraska, Fort Bliss (Texas), and Okinawa. And then it was back to Fort Bliss, Okinawa, Fort Bliss again, and then to New Jersey. My last duty station was in Germany. I was stationed in all those places within thirteen years.

The place I remember the most or the place I liked the most was Okinawa, Japan. I was sent to Okinawa in 1967. At that time, the United States still claimed the Ryukyu Islands because of the Japanese war. I spent two tours in Okinawa. Each tour was eighteen months.

The first time I landed on the island of Okinawa, we were quarantined for fourteen days. We were told that diseases were rampant, and we had to be very careful.

I was stationed on a missile site way up in the mountains, but where I was, I could see the ocean.

It was a beautiful tropical island. Some of the guys and I went sightseeing. We toured most of the villages in the area, but the one I liked was a village called Naminoue. It had a few restaurants, some quaint little shops, and a couple of bars.

At that time, I was a heavy drinker, and I loved women. I was always getting in trouble. It seemed like every payday, the MPs would have to bring me back to the base. I pulled a lot of duty, especially as sergeant of the guard. I was a sergeant (E-5), and security was a must. We had to guard the area twenty-four hours a day.

The missile site was underground, and there were three sections: A, B, and C. I was in charge of the B section. I believe I had ten or twelve men under me. I'm not bragging, but we had the best section. Whenever we had an inspection, the inspectors were always sent to our section.

We even had General Westmoreland tour our site. He was in charge of the Far East troops back in the sixties.

There was one bar that I took an interest in. The owner of the bar and I became good friends. She had a driver, and sometimes she had him take me back to the missile site early in the morning, before roll call. I was the only soldier that was allowed upstairs. Sometimes I would stay over the weekend.

There was a cave just outside the village overlooking the ocean. The winos stayed there. On occasion, I would visit them. We would sit around the campfire, eat, drink, and just look out over the ocean.

When we went on maneuvers, there was a place where we always practiced. Its name was Bolo Point. It was at the edge of the island, on a hill overlooking the ocean.

One time, we went to Bolo Point to practice riot control. It was raining so hard that we could hardly see. We had our ponchos, but our captain would not let us put them on. Boy did we get drenched. The colonel came out to see how we were doing. When he saw us without our ponchos, he chewed the captain out and told him he did not want to see that again.

There was more than one missile site on the island. Each site had twelve to fifteen men trained in riot control. From time to time, there were demonstrations. The missile sites had nuclear warheads on some of the missiles, and most of the people did not like that. The military police put the village off limits. I don't know why, but I slipped into the village.

I was walking down the street when two MPs appeared. I started running from them. I ran down an alley and tried to jump over a trash can. I must have passed out because when I woke up, I was on my back with my legs draped over the trash can. Ha ha. Anyway, I avoided the police that night.

The restriction finally ended, and everything went back to normal. On one account early one morning, I and a friend were looking for a bar to open. Someone forgot and left the front door to a bar unlocked, so we opened up the bar. We were sitting at the bar, having a drink, when the owner walked in. Ha ha. She was really surprised to see us. I paid for the drinks we had, and everything was just fine.

One night, I got into an argument with the Ryukyu police. They started beating me with their nightsticks. They were hitting me in the back and sides. The Okinawan police could not knock me down, so they started hitting my legs. I finally dropped to my knees. Luckily, the MPs (military police) stopped them.

I caught a cab and went back to the base. For two weeks, I was badly bruised, and I could barely move.

Of course, there was always something going on at the missile site. One time, just before an inspection, we loaded up a truck to hide some things that we didn't want the inspectors to see. I was still drunk from the night before, so they put me in the truck. There was a cave where everything was hidden, even me. Ha ha.

Some of the guys smoked pot. I did some, but that wasn't my bag.

Sometimes, late at night, I would catch a cab and go to the village.

From the barracks, we could see the ocean. Off in the distance, there was a small island. We were told that it was a leper colony.

At high tide, a person could only get to the island by boat; but at low tide, you could walk out to the island. I spent my first eighteen months on the island of Okinawa.

When I left, I was stationed at Fort Bliss in Texas. I put in my papers to spend another tour in Okinawa.

Four months later, I returned to the island. The same thing applied, and I was quarantined for fourteen days. But I slipped out of the barracks and went to the village of Naminoue. As I entered the bar, everyone was glad to see me back.

In 1968, someone by the name of Ronnie Fray wrote and recorded a song called "The Road to Naminoue."

I got the nickname the Naminoue Kid. I left Okinawa in 1971. I tried to return for a third tour, but the army wouldn't do it that time.

I believe in 1972, the United States gave the islands back to Japan, and the missile sites were closed. I never returned to Okinawa. I was in my twenties then, and I'm seventy-nine years old now.

It's been thirty-one years since I have had a drink. I think back to a time when I was on the island of Okinawa and the guys I was stationed with. Okinawa was an island paradise with good people and friends, and the nickname I was given was the Naminoue Kid.